JUNIOR BIOGRAPHIES

Hannah Isbell

RIHANNA
POP STAR

Enslow Publishing
101 W. 23rd Street
Suite 240
New York, NY 10011
USA

enslow.com

album—A collection of songs on a CD or record.

audition—To try out.

debut—An artist's first song or album.

demo—A piece of music that demonstrates, or shows, a new artist's talent and abilities.

genuine—Real, honest, and true.

icon—A person who is seen as a symbol of something.

producer—A person who is responsible for helping to manage and support an artist.

record label—A company that produces albums.

reggae—A style of music that began in Jamaica and became famous in the late 1960s.

single—A song released on its own.

soca—A blend of soul and calypso music that began in Trinidad.

studio—The space where an artist works.

CONTENTS

Rihanna

Rihanna is known the world over as a pop icon. She is famous not only for her singing but also for her genuine nature and ever-changing style. She was born by the sea on a small island. She worked as a child to help support her family and was often ill. But her talent and hard work helped her rise to stardom. She has released eight albums, appeared in movies and on TV, and made a name for herself as one of the most successful music artists of all time. Now she is able to help poor and sick children herself!

GROWING UP IN THE CARIBBEAN

Rihanna's full name is Robyn Rihanna Fenty. She was born on February 20, 1988, in Saint Michael, Barbados.

Rihanna Says:

"Music is in my DNA."

Rihanna's parents, Monica and Ronald, walk the red carpet in 2014.

She was raised in Bridgetown. As a child she learned the importance of hard work by selling clothes with her father in a street stall. She had five brothers and sisters to help support!

Rihanna's father struggled with alcohol and drug addiction, and she had a hard time. As a young teenager she began to have terrible headaches from stress, but things got better for her after her parents separated. Even though her family life was

Before leaving school and her home country of Barbados to pursue her music career, Rihanna was an army cadet. Singer-songwriter Shontelle was her drill sergeant!

hard, she often speaks about the importance of family and her devotion to them.

ROBYN REDBREAST

Rihanna loved music from the start. She grew up listening to Caribbean music like **soca** and **reggae**. Musician Bob Marley had a big influence on her. She also loved American pop, and artists like Whitney Houston and Madonna inspired her to start singing. By the age of seven, she was performing songs for her neighbors using a hairbrush as a pretend microphone. Her neighbors said she was like a songbird, giving her the nickname Robyn Redbreast.

Bob Marley was a Jamaican singer-songwriter who made reggae music popular in the 1960s and '70s. Rihanna often says he is one of her biggest influences.

CHAPTER 2
BECOMING A STAR

When Rihanna was still in school she formed a music group with two of her classmates. Together they sang for an American **producer**, Evan Rogers, who was visiting Barbados in search of fresh talent. Right away it was clear that Rihanna was the star. Rogers said, "The minute Rihanna walked into the room, it was like the other two girls didn't exist."

Rogers was so impressed with Rihanna that he flew her to the United States during her school holidays to record **demos**. Those demos helped to launch her career.

Rihanna Says:
"I'm a child but I have to think and act like a woman. This business forces you to."

Rihanna signs autographs in 2005, the year her first album was released.

TAKING OFF

Rihanna's demos were sent to **record labels** around the world, and she was soon invited to **audition** for rapper Jay Z, the owner of the label Def Jam. At first he was worried that she was too young and did not have enough experience. But Rihanna bowled him over with her talent. He was so worried another label would snatch her up that he made her wait all night until he could find lawyers to write up a contract!

In 2005, Rihanna released her first album, *Music of the Sun*. The single "Pon de Replay" was an instant smash hit. She blended dancehall reggae with pop and jazzy rhythms, making for a truly one of a kind sound. From

Rihanna has called pop star Madonna one of her greatest influences. Madonna changed what people expected from female artists and is constantly updating her style, just like Rihanna!

there, Rihanna's career took off like a rocket. In 2006, she recorded her second album, *A Girl Like Me*, went on her first tour, and even made her acting **debut**. By 2007, she was popular around the world, and had been nominated for several Grammy Awards.

Rihanna performs in Tokyo in 2007.

Rihanna shows off her trophy after winning the Grammy for Record of the Year for "Umbrella."

A NEW LIFE

During this time, Rihanna had to adjust to living in
a new country. She also had to take on many of the
responsibilities of an adult, even though she was still very
young. Rihanna worked hard, though, and rose to the
challenge. She won her first Grammy when she was only
nineteen years old!

CHAPTER 3
SHOPPING FOR SOUND

In the United States, Rihanna discovered music that was unlike anything she listened to as a child. She became a huge fan of rock music and R&B. She loves learning new things, saying, "I like to be taught, I like to be on that side of the table." As she learned about different kinds of music she began to blend the styles into her own work, while always respecting her Caribbean roots.

STYLE AND SOUND

Rihanna loves changing up her fashion style as much as she loves changing up her musical style. She has become known for her love of fashion, treating it as a form of

Rihanna has worked with some of music's biggest stars. She has performed with hip-hop artists, rappers, rock bands, and pop stars. Drake, Eminem, Kanye West, Coldplay, and Paul McCartney are just a few of the artists and bands she has worked with.

Rihanna performs with Chris Martin of Coldplay at the closing ceremony of the 2012 London Paralympics.

art. She even draws musical inspiration from changing her look. She cut her hair while recording her album *Good Girl Gone Bad* in 2007. She said that doing so completely changed her style as a singer.

Rihanna has said that she wasn't happy being a pop princess and wanted to be different. Reinventing her style is part of what keeps her unique and fresh as a music star. She has been compared to some of the biggest fashion icons in music history, including Madonna, David Bowie, and Prince.

Rihanna Says:

"Music is like shopping for me. Every song is like a new pair of shoes. I love these, have these, these look great —but what's new?"

Rihanna, shown here at the 2015 Met Gala in New York City, uses fashion to express herself artistically.

CHAPTER 4
TAKING CONTROL

The true secret to Rihanna's success isn't her look or even her talent as a singer, but her hard work. She spends most of her time in the studio working and feels strongly about taking control of her music, image, and career. She controls her own social media and devotes much of her energy to charity. Along with performing charity concerts for people with cancer and HIV/AIDS, she created her own charity, Believe Foundation, to help terminally ill children.

Rihanna Says:

"They're gonna keep knocking away until all this comes crashing down. But I'm not gonna ever crash. I'm in control."

Rihanna and Prince Harry attend an HIV/AIDS charity event in Barbados.

NOT A ROLE MODEL

Rihanna speaks often about the importance of being true to herself, to her Caribbean roots, and about being genuine with her fans. People often say that she is easy

Rihanna performs in
Italy in 2016.

to get along with and very down to earth, despite her star status. She often points out her own imperfections and mistakes. She has said many times that she doesn't think of herself as a role model. However, her honesty and hard work are definitely worth looking up to!

Rihanna is the youngest solo artist to chart fourteen number one singles, and she did so faster than any other artist. She has also sold over 200 million records worldwide!

TIMELINE

1988 Robyn Rihanna Fenty is born in Saint Michael, Barbados.

2004 Auditions for Jay Z and Def Jam.

2005 Releases first album, *Music of the Sun.*

2006 Releases second album, *A Girl Like Me*, and goes on first tour.

2006 Creates her Believe Foundation to help terminally ill children.

2007 Wins her first Grammy for the song "Umbrella" from the album *Good Girl Gone Bad.*

2010 Rihanna's vocal performance is praised in her fifth studio album, *Loud.*

2015 Rihanna stands up for the LGBTQ+ community at the NCAA March Madness Music Festival.

2016 Releases her eighth studio album, *Anti.* Becomes "the first black face of Dior," modeling and designing for the brand.

Learn More

Books

Harringshaw, Dianne. *Rihanna: Grammy-Winning Superstar.* Edina, MN: Abdo Publishing, 2014.

Johnson, Robin. *Rihanna.* New York, NY: Crabtree, 2013.

Saddleback Educational Publishing. *Rihanna.* Costa Mesa, CA: Saddleback, 2013.

Websites

MTV Artists: Rihanna

www.mtv.com/artists/rihanna

Watch music videos and interviews plus photos and biography.

Rihanna Now

www.rihannanow.com

Rihanna's official website where you can find photos, fashion, and news.

Published in 2018 by Enslow Publishing, LLC
101 W. 23rd Street, Suite 240 New York, NY 10011

Library of Congress Cataloging-in-Publication Data

Names: Isbell, Hannah, author.
Title: Rihanna : pop star / Hannah Isbell.
Description: New York : Enslow Publishing, 2018. | Series: Junior biographies
  | Includes bibliographical references and index. | Audience: Grades 3-5.
Identifiers: LCCN 2017003124| ISBN 9780766086746 (library-bound) | ISBN
  9780766087835 (pbk.) | ISBN 9780766087842 (6-pack)
Subjects: LCSH: Rihanna, 1988– —Juvenile literature. | Singers—Biography—Juvenile literature.
Classification: LCC ML3930.R44 I38 | DDC 782.42164092 [B] —dc23
LC record available at https://lccn.loc.gov/2017003124

Printed in the United States of America

To Our Readers: We have done our best to make sure all websites in this book were active and appropriate when we went to press. However, the author and the publisher have no control over and assume no liability for the material available on those websites or on any websites they may link to. Any comments or suggestions can be sent by e-mail to customerservice@enslow.com.

Photo Credits: Cover, p. 1 Tinseltown/Shutterstock.com; pp. 4, 6 Jon Kopaloff/FilmMagic/Getty Images; p. 7 Michael Ochs Archives/Getty Images; p. 9 Brad Barket/Getty Images; p. 11 Junko Kimura/Getty Images; p. 12 AFP/Getty Images; p. 15 Peter Macdiarmid/Getty Images; p. 17 Karwai Tang/WireImage/Getty Images; p. 19 Chris Jackson/Getty Images; p. 20 Mondadori Portfolio/Getty Images; pp. 2, 3, 22, 23, 24 (curves graphic) Alena Kazlouskaya/Shutterstock.com; interior pages (colored lights) Florian Augustin/Shutterstock.com.